ABERDEEN & THE NORTH EAST AT WAR

PAUL HARRIS

LOMOND BOOKS

First published by Archive Publications Ltd. 1987

Reprinted 1995 by Lomond Books
36 West Shore Road
Granton
Edinburgh

Printed in the Republic of Slovenia by Gorenjski Tisk Printing Co., Kranj

The front page of a special edition of the **Evening Express** of Sunday, September 3 1939

CONTENTS

INTRODUCTION

WAR IS DECLARED

CIVIL DEFENCE

THE HOME GUARD

THE GORDON HIGHLANDERS

AIR FORCES AT DYCE & PETERHEAD

HMS *ABERDEEN* & HMS *SCYLLA*

THE BOMBING

INDUSTRY AT WAR

PETERHEAD & FRASERBURGH

THE HOME FRONT

VICTORY !

THE ABERDEEN VICTORIA CROSS

BIBLIOGRAPHY

ACKNOWLEDGEMENTS

Many people have helped with this book and I should particularly like to thank those who gave of their time and encouragement so generously: Harry Roulston, Editor of the *Press & Journal*, and his assistant, Ranald Allan, who have been so enthusiastic in their support for this project; David Sutherland, Picture Editor of the *P & J*, and Bob Bruce who were so helpful in "digging out" the wartime glass plates from which most of these pictures came; Tommy Forsyth and his colleagues for foraging in the library of the paper; the National Library of Scotland and Aberdeen District Libraries for access to contemporary newspapers; Miss Judith Cripps for access to the City archives and the Hall Russell pictures, and Miss Frazer of Hall Russell & Co Ltd (pictures 97—108); Captain Colin Harrison of the Gordon Highlanders for research assistance and pictures 71, 72; the Imperial War Museum for pictures 66—70; and to Nigel Arthur and Clive Hardy for their skilled detective work, specifically on the air force and Victory Cup photographs.

Paul Harris
May 1987

"Man's inhumanity to Man
Makes countless thousands mourn"
Robert Burns

INTRODUCTION

I was speaking recently to a writer who prided himself on his proficiency in his chosen field: books on the Second World War. I told him I was putting together this present book, *Aberdeen & the North East at War.* He looked bemused, "What war?", quoth he, and he was genuinely amazed when I told him something of the experiences of the north east during that period of war from 1939-45.

I suppose that for the vast majority of people the Second World War experience in Scotland is synonymous with the Clydebank Blitz of April, 1941, when two nights of attack by massed bombers left only a dozen houses in that bustling Clydeside community undamaged. Yet, just as that image ignores the much greater toll wrought on the City of Glasgow as a whole during the war years, it also represents an inadequate appreciation of the effects of the war on communities outwith the central belt of Scotland. Even the Scottish Office (or the Office of the Regional Commissioner for Scotland as it was then) did not expect attacks on any great scale in the north east of the country and no plans were ever made to take over the administration in the north as they were for central Scotland. Indeed, the reports of the District Commissioner were not even submitted to Edinburgh but instead went direct to the Home Office in London. You can search in the Scottish Records Office in vain for any reference to a war ever having taken place in Aberdeen—for there is none. In short, the absence of recognition for what was a very hard war for Aberdeen and the north east is virtually total and is quite simply a travesty of the actual truth.

For the incontrovertible fact is that the war touched virtually every family in the north east and most often violently and shockingly. Aberdeen itself was the most

bombed city in Scotland in terms of the number of attacks mounted over a three year period, and the havoc wrought on Peterhead and Faserburgh, for towns of their size, was truly terrible. Curiously, there is little in print of this wartime experience.

The official HMSO publication *FRONT LINE 1940-41; the official story of the civil defence of Britain* (1942) does give some clue to the official concern for the coastal towns in the chapter entitled 'Seaside Tip-and-Run':

> Many of the coastal towns were (and are) bombed all the time . . . a knowledge of the coast and what is happening there is important to the enemy on several grounds . . . he reconnoitred it continually. Reconnaissance planes carry bombs . . . minelaying is a dull and boring job, and the German crews carried a bomb or two for launching as a treat, or to relieve their feelings: the coastal towns were (and are) the victims . . . planes on the hunt for shipping treated the small seaside towns as alternative targets . . . not all these places were heavily defended: any irresolute crew could bomb them in comparative safety and then go home to report Fierce Fires and Great Explosions.

The coastal towns of the Channel were obviously the prime targets. Although the north east casualty figures were small numerically, they were vast in relation to the populations of small towns like Peterhead and Fraserburgh. Yet these continued and sustained attacks were met with a resilience matching that of the now legendary Londoner in the blitz.

It must be pointed out, though, that the term 'blitz' should not be applied to the north east: the Blitz begins

The **Press & Journal** of Friday September 1 1939

The **Press & Journal** of Saturday September 2 1939

in Britain on September 9 1940 with the first great aerial bombardment on London, continues through with the great attack on Coventry on November 14 of that year (which itself gave birth to that graphic and descriptive term 'Coventration') and other great attacks on the Midlands of England. The detailed chronicler of aerial attack on Britain Tom Harrisson, in his classic book *Living Through the Blitz*, is drawn to define a 'blitz' as an attack involving "over 100 piloted bombers . . . at one conurbation on one night". Sustained and damaging though the attacks on the north east were, blitzes they were not.

But this is to jump ahead somewhat in the story. Just a few hours after the declaration of war on September 3, the SS *Athenia* was sunk 200 miles west of the Hebrides. The whole country was shocked by the brutal sinking of the passenger ship and the news came hard to the north east, carrying as she did a number of people from the area.

On September 17 survivors of the *Truro* were brought ashore at Aberdeen — the first torpedoed crew to land in the north east. From that point on, every few days, torpedoed, mined or bombed survivors were to arrive at north east ports in a steady stream. And then, of course, the north east learned with dismay the following month of the sinking of the *Royal Oak* by a Nazi U-boat within the very defences of Scapa Flow and with the loss of 800 lives.

On November 28 the Aberdeen steamship *Rubislaw* was sunk in the North Sea and thirteen men drowned. On January 21 1940 another local ship, the *Ferryhill* was sunk (earlier in the month a ship had been bombed and sunk off Girdleness within sight of the city).

The first tangible indication of war for Aberdeen was the evacuation which started on September 1st 1939. That day, the *Press & Journal* reported that, "The North of Scotland is ready to receive today the first of its tens of thousands of evacuees from the evacuation areas" and within just three days Aberdeenshire was, indeed, to receive 30,000 children and 10,000 adults — many from Glasgow and Clydebank. More than 30 trains arrived on one single day at the joint station and on September 1st alone 14 special trains took 4,000 mothers and children on to Aboyne, whilst Kincardineshire received thousands of evacuees from Dundee. No children were evacuated from Aberdeen itself — the city was designated, somewhat over optimistically, as a "neutral area". The extraordinary thing is how smoothly — by and large — this major operation went although the *Press and Journal* was to regretfully record that Strathdon parents were protesting about their children being taught along with Roman Catholic children from Glasgow. The problems arising from this lack of enlightenment were shortlived: by November 22nd the newspaper was reporting that "half the Scots evacuees are back home". Indeed, most of those children decanted from the major Scots cities into the imagined safety and tranquillity of the countryside returned home as the Phoney War set in; and the massive aerial bombardments typified by Baldwin's prediction, "The bomber will always get through", failed to materialise.

During those first few weeks of war the sight of soldiers marching off to war via Union Street and the joint station became a regular one. The atmosphere was nonchalant if not exactly carnival. The newspapers were coy about these movements, under the influence of censorship introduced at the end of the first week in September. A photograph of the Gordon Highlanders marching off to war from Aberdeen, past plainly identifiable landmarks, is blandly captioned, "A well known Scottish regiment on the march", and a picture at Aberdeen station becomes merely, "A typical wartime scene at a Scottish station". How irritating this must have seemed to newspaper readers of the time. And puzzled and perceptive readers of the *P & J* are counselled, "Lack of News does Not Mean Lack of Action".

The so-called 'Phoney War' period did bring some extraordinary stories into the paper. On October 13, a page 1 story announces, "Month in prison for flashing a torch" and a few days later readers are advised, "Don't look up during an air raid. A lighted match can be seen 10,000 feet away".

But, late in October 1939, the effects of war become more threatening as news filters through of attacks on shipping in the North Sea. On October 17 the Royal Mail ship *St. Ola* is attacked on passage between Thurso and Scapa, and fishing boats and trawlers are now under attack.

On November 1 there was a false alarm (caused by a short circuit) in Aberdeen. This showed up some serious

The **Press & Journal** of Monday September 4 1939

The war is on! Removing the cannons from in front of Robert Gordon's College

failings. The musical "A Desert Song" was being performed at His Majesty's Theatre at the time and the *P & J* representative present recorded that "Not one member of the audience made a move to leave the theatre"!

The following month, apart from reporting the increasing popularity of venison sausages, readers were, more alarmingly, advised that 7 Nazi planes had been seen off Aberdeen (December 8). In the third week of December the Grimsby trawler *Etruria* was dive bombed off Aberdeen and three of her crew killed before she managed to reach shelter within Aberdeen Harbour. Attacks on shipping intensified early in 1940. The neutral Danish steamer *Feddy* was attacked within sight of the coast, fishing vessels were now regularly mined or attacked by planes in the North Sea and, in March 1940, Queen Elizabeth was moved to praise the efforts of fishermen when she visited Aberdeen — the very same day as a two-man yawl from Fraserburgh, the *Sisters*, was bombed 7 miles off the port setting some sort of a new low in terms of strategic targets. Meantime, on January 26 1940, the first German bombs had been dropped on the north east in the grounds of Tullos House, Nigg, although the first raid involving serious loss of life was not to occur until July 12 1940 when 34 people were killed in a daylight raid on Aberdeen.

Aberdonians had already been made conscious of the fact that they were in the frontline with the collapse of Norway in May 1940. Thousands of Norwegian refugees crossed the North Sea in small boats and for them the north east was the nearest landfall. But it was the fall of Holland, Belgium and France which was to bring, in June 1940, the catastrophic loss of so many men of the 51st Highland Division, including two battalions of the Gordon Highlanders, at St. Valery. At one disastrous stroke the cream of north east youth was lost in a crippling blow in which hardly a family in the area was spared. The remnants of the 51st came back to the north east for reconstruction and it was a considerable tribute to its valiant efforts in northern France that the War Office immediately ordered the Division's reconstitution.

By contrast, when there was good news to report it was received ecstatically. On August 2 1940 the SS *Highlander* steamed into an "East of Scotland" port — Aberdeen — with the wreckage of a Heinkel on her poop deck, having the day previously shot two of them down with her Lewis Gun.

It was a feature of newspaper coverage at the time that, by and large, photographs of local bomb damage were not printed in the paper — presumably so as not to undermine morale and as a result of cooperation between the censor and the newspaper. Many such photographs were actually taken but few used in the *Press & Journal*. London air raid pictures were frequently used and an early, solitary, bomb damage picture was published on August 29 1940 showing the home of Mrs Shirriffs in Forbesfield Road. This was reported at the time simply as damage "in a NE town", as was a picture of a raid on Peterhead on September 30.

On November 6 1940 the headline proclaimed, "Seven killed by bombs in NE Town" and extensive damage caused by three enemy aircraft was reported. This was, in fact, the notorious raid on Fraserburgh when Nazi planes were guided to the town by a fire at Benzie & Miller's department store; a bomb then hit a public house where a darts match was taking place and it is recorded that a plane tried to drop bombs on the crowd watching the big department store blaze.

Stories of wartime events are sometimes distinctly bizarre. One, from December 1940, headlined dramatically "Back from the Dead" and told the story of Aberdeen seaman James Burnett of the Royal Naval Reserve. James, of 60 Mansefield Place, was reported dead — "buried at sea" — by the Admiralty in May 1940. A death certificate duly followed and Mrs Burnett remarried. Then, to the discomfiture of all involved, a letter arrived the following December from a German POW camp from — you guessed it — James Burnett, reporting himself alive and well. Mrs Burnett's comments were not recorded — neither is there any indication as to how this unholy mess was sorted out!

Jokes about the Home Guard are clearly not just a postwar phenomenon. At Aberdeen Sheriff Court, in September 1940, Home Guardsman Robert Pratt had his case dismissed when he was charged with breaking the jaw of one Ernest Tough of Bridge of Don. Tough, apparently, had made reference in the bar of the Potarch Hotel to "a puckle of low down volunteers" being present — a facetious play on the LDVs. But the Sheriff opined, "The man got what he deserved".

Thus the tragic and the bizarre mix side by side in the columns of the wartime press. For a while, there was actually a column in the *P & J* with the colourful title of "Air Raid Splinters" — a sort of morale boosting round-up of news about bombings in towns all over Britain (except Aberdeen, that is). As the war goes on, however, the pressure of space in newspapers becomes acute and by the beginning of 1942 the *P & J* is reduced to a mere 4 pages and so 'serious' news becomes a more real citerion.

The encirclement and capture of the men of the 51st Highland Division in June 1940 brought home to people in the north east the plight of POWs in enforced capitivity — possibly for a very long time. In September 1940 the *P & J* invited readers "Help N. E. Men in Hands of the Enemy" and started a 'war comforts fund' to raise money for weekly food parcels for prisoners. Alas, the blow of St. Valery was to be repeated again in the early months of 1942 when the 2nd Gordons were captured in the surrender of Singapore and, also, scores of north east families were reported missing when the Japanese overran the Peninsular.

Without a doubt, the blackest night of the war for Aberdeen was the night of Wednesday April 21 1943. The city had been spared a large scale, planned attack by the Luftwaffe although there had been constant tip-and-run raids. Indeed, a false sense of security had set in in official circles and, only the week before, most of the city's anti-aircraft guns had been rushed south in the aftermath of attacks in the south.

That day 25 aircraft of the Kampf-Geschwader Group 2, stationed at Soesterberg near Utrecht in Holland, were ordered to fly to Stavanger. There the planes — Dornier 217s — were refuelled, armed and took on over two tons of bombs each. The orders then came form Luftwaffe Headquarters in Berlin: the target was Aberdeen. As dusk fell in Aberdeen, shortly after nine in the evening, the planes swept in from the north with devastating effect. The Woodside, Hilton, Kittybrewster and George Street areas were particularly badly hit. Middlefield School, Causewayend Church, Carden Place Episcopal Church, the Royal Mental Hospital, the nurses' home and the Gordon Barracks were all bombed and set alight. A *Press & Journal* reporter watched from the rooftop of his office in Broad Street:

It seemed they were out to attack big buildings and densely populated areas. Their phosphorous and oil bombs started fires and they unloaded their high explosive bombs in the vicinity of the blazing buildings . . . In Woodside and Hilton bungalows and tenements were wiped out, and a plane roaring over the rooftops in Kittybrewster landed a bomb close to a shelter in which 13 railwaymen had taken refuge (4 died). It collapsed. Not far away three bungalows simply vanished and a tenement crumbled with a number of families inside.

One bomb tore an enormous hole in the front of Causewayend Church. Another dropped in the grounds of Robert Gordon's College and yet another scored a direct hit on a school in George Street. Luckily, in the night nursery next door all the children escaped with cuts.

Other planes attacked with cannon and machine guns blazing and a bus was attacked. Streets were raked with bullets. The whole of the north end of George Street to 'Split the Wind' was a mass of fires. A reporter, writing on May 20, almost a month later, after a decent interval had elapsed, described how, "Down the back streets wound sad, straggling little processions of homeless old men and women and mothers with crying babies being shepherded to the rest centres."

The Meat Mart was hit but the staff extinguished the blaze with stirrup pumps. A house in Charles Street was less lucky — it "flared like a beacon". A stick of bombs fell in St Peter's Cemetery and blew out glass all over the seaward side of the City. "In Ashvale Place a police sergeant and I surveyed a tenement that was now just a pile of stones. 'Out of there', the sergeant said, 'We took three stretcher cases and seven walking cases. Not a man, woman or child was killed.'"

The Wilkes family of Summer Street received high praise for rescuing their neighbours, the Philips, despite the attentions of machine guns.

One hero of the night was Mr Frank Newman of Charles Street, a fire guard leader. His home received a direct hit. He found his wife in the derbis just as she died. Beside her lay his daughter Barbara — dead. Three other daughters and his grandson all lost their lives when their home crashed in on them. The daughters had been standing by as fire guards ready with stirrup pumps.

Despite this appalling ordeal, Mr Newman went on to rescue two children of a neighbour who were buried in debris.

In Powis Place and Fraser Road, nearby, others were more lucky as the local surface shelter withstood the blasts of three high explosive bombs.

The toll of that terrible night was heavy: 98 people were killed, 93 seriously injured and 141 with minor injuries. Eight thousand houses were damaged of which 599 were rendered uninhabitable.

A curious after-effect of the raid was noted. It seems that many people had been hoarding money at home and a rush to the banks started. Within a fortnight more than £75,000 had been deposited at Aberdeen Savings Bank.

Fortunately, there was never again a raid on this scale. Luftwaffe bombing raids had failed to break morale in the civilian population of Britain and the failure of this strategy brought attention to other targets. By all accounts Aberdonians were characteristically matter of fact in their response to air raids such as this. The common sense response of one north easter was quoted at the time: "Aye, we can stick it. Fit else is there tae dee?"

And first thing the next morning there was an energetic figure out in the streets of Aberdeen surveying the damage, assessing the situation and giving encouragement . . .

The man to whom the credit must go for guiding Aberdeen through the dark days of the war is Lord Provost Thomas Mitchell. A spry figure with a pawky sense of humour, he was extremely popular at all levels in the City. Of humble origins — he started life as an apprentice in a little bakery in Daviot — he became Lord Provost in 1938. On June 2 1943 he was knighted in recognition of his services to the its community. The P & J commented:

> Lord Provost Mitchell has kept in close touch with all the wartime activities of the city and has carried through his duties with a characteristic initiative and energy. He has always made tours of damaged areas immediately after raids and he championed the interests of the trawlermen in those early war days when they suffered from air attacks.

Lord Provost Mitchell helped as much as anybody to dispel the myth of the meanness of the Aberdonian for he was always in the forefront of wartime fundraising. In Wings for Victory Week, in June 1943, Aberdeen raised war investments totalling £870,888 in the first two days alone and, by the end of the week, the total had reached £3,256,528.

The Lord Provost launched an appeal to buy three Spitfires and so enthusiastic were the much bombed Aberdonians that £20,000 — enough for four — was raised. They were called *Bon Accord, Cock o' the North, Bydand* and *Dunnottar Castle.*

In Warship Week Aberdeen set out to raise £2,700,000 and, in fact, over £3m. was achieved and he was cheered roundly by the men of H M S *Scylla* when he told them how "Aberdeen's siller" had built their ship. 'Tommy' Mitchell was Aberdeen's much loved Lord Provost for a total of nine years, covering the entire Second War period and lived on to the ripe age of 90. He died in August 1959.

As if the wartime depradations of enemy aircraft were not enough, many towns and fishing villages on the north east coast had to contend with the threat of mines, cast adrift and blown ashore. In late 1944 there was havoc on the Kincardineshire coast when severe easterly gales tore mines from their moorings in the North Sea and cast them ashore.

Especially badly hit was Stonehaven where one mine actually drifted between the pierheads and into the north basin of Stonehaven Harbour on November 15. That lunchtime the entire harbour area was evacuated and the inhabitants looked down on the scene from the Bervie Braes. Shortly before nightfall the mine exploded, blowing a hole in the harbour wall, wrecking a house on the Shorehead occupied by a Mrs Main and blowing the roofs off many others. The force of the blast even blew people off their feet in the High Street but it is recorded that despite all this a 94-year-old lady, Mrs Smart, living only 60 yards away resolutely refused to leave her home!

All the windows in the Marine Hotel were blown in and half a mile away in Market Square the plate glass

The **Evening Express** helps the war effort. A paper van hauls Home Guard armament

windows in Provost Hugh Ramsay's drapery shop were blown in.

Other mines grounded near Turner's Close and Allardice Street and at Bridge of Cowie. There were explosions throughout the night of November 16 but the damage was not as serious as that first explosion within the harbour.

Along a twenty mile stretch of the Kincardineshire coast mines exploded against rocks and harbour walls. At Catterline three mines exploded in the cove below the village breaking windows and damaging roofs. There were also explosions at Cove Bay and Newtonhill on the night of November 17.

There was much fear of spies, fifth columnists and saboteurs of the war effort. A great deal of quite uncalled for paranoia was released by Churchill's expression of fifth columnist fears, "This malignancy in our midst". Although this did serve to alert people to the fact that careless talk could indeed cost lives, such fears were largely overdone as the proprietors of ice cream parlours and fish and chip shops were interned on a wholesale basis and such a rigid press censorship was introduced that at times people came to positively distrust the press.

Former Aberdeen police sergeant Kenny Cole recalls the gathering together of aliens in Aberdeen. "In a city the size of Aberdeen we knew them all personally and had a pretty good idea whether or not they were going to help Hitler. They were all decent enough folk."

Lord Haw Haw was listened to avidly although many of his pronouncements were patently ludicrous. "The British nation (sic) has taken to drink," he blithely advised. "We had — long before the Nazis," countered J B Priestley. But he obviously did have *some* accurate sources of information. Within days of the landing at Peterhead of a quantity of fresh fruit — a prize of war — William Joyce was on the radio suggesting that people of Peterhead should be grateful to Hitler for the gift.

The north east had its own answer to Lord Haw Haw. Professor Lindley Fraser, Professor of Political Economy at Aberdeen University, broadcast via the facilities of the BBC to the people of Germany. The *Press & Journal* reported: "Information reaching this country in recent weeks shows that the Professor is attracting in Germany a much greater radio audience than the notorious Lord Haw Haw has ever achieved here" (*P & J* October 11 1940). Apparently, the Professor's detailed knowledge of Germany and the German mentality, allied to his fluency in the language, was having a considerable effect. "Evidence has reached this country that the enemy's propaganda service is vastly concerned about the professor".

Again, Kenny Cole remembers: "We had set up Bofors guns on the promenade but the bombers always avoided it. So we took them all away. The next night the bombers flew right over the promenade . . . Somebody was sending information from here to Germany but we never found out who."

Lord Provost Thomas Mitchell

The Germans *did* land spies in the north east. None were perhaps as obvious as the one, remembered by Malcolm Muggeridge, who had apparently educated himself in the matter of English life from P G Wodehouse and who landed in the Fen country actually wearing a bowler and spats! But three mysterious characters who turned up in Portgordon in September 1940, buying rail tickets to London via Forres, had on their persons when searched a thick German blood sausage, a radio transmitter, a Mauser and a list of bomber and fighter stations!

These characters, it turned out, had come ashore in a rubber dinghy from a submarine. Two others who landed at Gardenstown were spotted as strangers by the locals and arrested as they bicycled south.

The now well-known Norwegian agent John Moe, landed by submarine in Banffshire in March 1941 together with colleague Tor Glad, were captured soon after landing and successfully 'turned' by MI5. Both became diligent double agents and sent false information to their Abwehr controllers for nearly four years. Unfortunately, in February 1943, one of their operations had a tragic end when they asked their German controllers to supply more equipment by air. A single Luftwaffe plane dropped a canister containing money and a transmitter in the north east but, on his way home, the German pilot decided to amuse himself by dropping a stick of bombs on the fishing port of Fraserburgh. An 11-year old boy was killed in the incident and Moe was extremely upset at this unlooked for diversion. The Abwehr undertook to stop the Luftwaffe repeating the exercise (believing it had caused problems for Moe's espionage operations), which was, unfortunately, all too typical of the continued tip-and-run raids the north east experienced.

In May 1943, the airport at Dyce was the centre for a remarkable covert operation when what has been described as a "factory fresh" Junkers 88 was landed on the tarmac and surrendered to the British war effort. The details are still secret to this day but what has been suspected is that dissident anti-Nazis in Germany arranged with the Allies for the defection of the aircraft, from a Danish base. The aircraft carried new airborne radar equipment developed for the Luftwaffe — knowledge of which was absolutely vital to our own anti-radar scientists like Professor R V Jones. The escort of the plane, with its top secret Lichtenstein radar equipment, into Dyce by two Spitfires, which met it off the Aberdeenshire coat, represented a considerable coup.

One of the more extraordinary stories of an Aberdonian at war must be that of Corporal W. Gray of the 2nd Battalion Gordon Highlanders who was captured by the Japanese on the fall of Singapore. In captivity, he was fortunate enough to acquire a duck which, although actually female, was not unreasonably christened, Donald. Unfortunately, the keeping of pets was strictly forbidden by the Camp Commandant and it looked as though halpless Donald would be put to the sword (or more likely the cooking pot). With great presence of mind, Corporal Gray advised the Japs that Donald was, in fact, a sacred duck held in great reverence by the prisoners and, to make their point, they went on their knees each morning to Donald! The Japs were duly impressed by this, the duck survived, lay 163 eggs whilst in captivity and ultimately returned home with his owner at the end of the war where, it is recorded, Donald mated with an Aberdeenshire duck and, allegedly, produced offspring with slit eyes!

WAR IS DECLARED

1   The Royal Scots Greys on the march in Aberdeen, July 1934.

The formal declaration of war on the morning of Sunday September 3 1939 scarcely came as a surprise. Planning for war had long been in hand — although people had hoped that it would not be necessary. The greatest fear was of the widespread damage and loss of life which, it was expected bombing would cause and, during that first weekend of September, 170,000 schoolchildren and mothers were 'spirited away' to the comparative safety of the country from Edinburgh, Dundee, Glasgow and Clydebank. The joint station at Aberdeen became a dispersal point for children and parents from Dundee and Glasgow who went on to the country (4-8). The twin marks of the evacuee were the identifying luggage label and a cardboard box containing the gas mask. 38 million gas masks had been distributed before the outbreak of war at a time when the possibility of gas attack was thought to be a real threat (9-13).

The anticipated gas and aerial attacks failed to develop and over the winter of 1939-40 an estimated three quarters of the evacuees were to return to their homes in the cities. Nevertheless, the actual evacuation was a miracle of organisation.

For the armed forces, this was to be a very different war from the First World War. The Royal Scots Greys riding through Aberdeen in 1934 (1) represented the old fashioned way of waging war. This new war was to be a mechanised one fought with all manner of new inventions. But as in the First War there was no lack of volunteers (16-20).

Even young pairs of hands set willingly to work filling sandbags (14) or collecting salvage (15). The Government discovered that children were the keenest collectors of salvage and initiated the 'Cog Scheme' appointing them as official salvage collectors or 'cogs'. The official 'Cog' song, "There'll always be a dustbin", was sung to the tune of "There'll always be an England" as they made their way through the streets.

As the first recruits set off for dispersal points and basic training there is as yet little hint of the long struggle which stretches ahead.

2 Recruiting for the Fish Trade Troop, Albert Quay, April 1939.

3 These potential recruits appear none too impressed!

4   September 1 1939 and evacuees leave the joint station at Aberdeen for the country. The children sport luggage labels for identification and carry their gas masks in cardboard boxes tied with string.

5   A roll call upon arrival at Banchory Station.

6   Evacuees leave Aberdeen by bus for schools on Deeside, September 1.

7   A young evacuee has his luggage label read at Banchory Station.

8   Evacuees at a Deeside school.

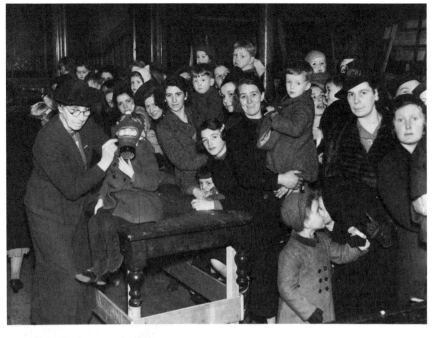

9

Gas mask distribution to children just before the outbreak of war.

10

A mother is shown the use of a baby respirator.

12 Gas mask distribution to adults.

11 Gas mask assembly and distribution.

13   An extraordinary sight — and, surely, stranger sound — at the telephone exchange during a gas mask drill.

14   Boys from Robert Gordon's College fill sandbags down at the harbour, September 4, just after the declaration of war. The North of Scotland Orkney and Shetland Steamship Co steamship "St Sunniva" is moored behind.

15   The Boys Brigade, led by three pipers, collect salvage for the war effort, September 1939.

16

At the beginning of October soldiers started to leave Aberdeen for training and dispersal camps. A rather relaxed group of Royal Engineers march down Union Street bound for the station.

17

The Royal Artillery departure, October 6, 1939.

18

The Royal Army Medical Corps bound for the station in Bridge Street, October 9.

Aberdeen Football club players Strauss, Armstrong and Cowie enlist for the Royal Corps of Signals at the Music Hall. Here they are handed their travel warrants.

20   The Royal Corps of Signals departure, October 9, for their dispersal point and, ultimately, Northern France.

CIVIL DEFENCE

21   Sandbags protect Police Headquarters at Lodge Walk.

The establishment of ARP arose out of Cabinet approval in 1935 for the spending of £100,000 on planning for the contingency of war. It was widely expected that aerial bombardment would start within hours, if not minutes, of the outbreak of war. By the end of 1938, 1.4 million people had joined ARP in the wake of the Munich crisis.

Most ARPs were wardens whose job it was at the beginning of the war to enforce the blackout and then, in the event of attack, to judge the extent and type of any damage in their particular area so that the local Control Centre could send appropriate rescue services. The local knowledge of the Wardens was vital in getting survivors out as quickly as possible. Once out, it was the further responsibility of the Warden to get survivors to a shelter or Rest Centre. More than 90% of Wardens were part-timers and around 20% were women.

Under the direction of the Control Centre were First Aid parties and Rescue Men. ARP also embraced the Women's Voluntary Service who manned canteens and Rest Centres.

The most important ARP work was preventative and involved the construction and provision of shelters (22-4) and sandbagging (21). At 6.30 p.m. on Friday September 1 the air raid warning sirens in Aberdeen were tested for the first time and throughout the war there were ARP tests (28-31, 34, 35) to ensure a constant state of preparedness.

Many ARP precautions and activities were misconceived or largely ineffective but were, nevertheless, effective from the point of view of morale. In the blackout, road deaths more than doubled and by January 1940 one person in four had suffered an accident in the blackout! In 1940, Lord Beaverbrook, in charge of aircraft production, appealed for aluminium pots and pans for transmogrification into Hurricanes and Spitfires (39). The appeal was unnecessary, as was the removal of iron railings and gates (36). Over a million tons of scrap iron was salvaged but little of it was ever used.

22   Building underground air raid shelters at Robert Gordon's College at the end of September, 1939.

23   A basic design of indoor shelter.

25   James Christie's specially built underground shelter at the bottom of his back garden in Tullos Circle. Mr. Christie is standing (centre, back).

26   Keep fit training for women territorials.

27   Searchlight training for territorials under a Battery Sergeant Major.

28

An ARP test in Union Street (June 1941). Smoke
bombs are set off and passers by — on foot or
bicycle — don gas masks.

29

Discomfort and inconvenience usually marked
ARP tests which were often not taken altogether
seriously.

30

An ARP exercise, December 1939.
Cleansing Department workers have
sand for extinguishing incendiaries and
water and masks for decontamination.

32   In July 1940 civil defence facilities under inspection, seen at the Castlegate Water Tank, left to right, Sir Douglas Thomson, MP (South Aberdeen), Lord Provost Thomas Mitchell, Garro Jones, MP (North Aberdeen), Chief Constable McCormack.

34   A fire service exercise. Note the use of canvas buckets and a stirrup pump.

35   ARP first aid exercise.

36   Ornamental iron railings are removed for scrap from graves at St Peter's Cemetery, July 1940.

'SAVE SCRAP' *BY ORDER*

Every Bit A Bullet, Says Minister

MUDLARKS AT ETON

Eton College boys have volunteered to do work of national service in factories, warehouses, and on the land on their half-holidays. Here are two Etonians clearing a stream—and appear to be enjoying it.

WEDDING FEAST WAS ON TABLE FOR 80 YEARS

A WEDDING breakfast was laid in the dining room of Mansfield House, Rochestown, County Cork. The daughter of the house was at the church, being married to a suitor whom the family approved. The servants, gossiping as they put the final touches to the festive table, remarked how pleased the parents were. . . . Remarked, also, that the bride seemed anything but pleased.

The wedding party came home. The bride retired to her room. The groom, apple of her family's eye, chatted easily with the assembled guests while

house (Mrs. Ethel Pike and others), who opposed, told how the wedding breakfast lay undisturbed from 1820 till 1904, when Mr. Clarke's father went into possession. Glass, china, cutlery,

'A WAR JOB'— AND IT'S COMPULSORY

"EVERY piece of paper, every old bone, every piece of scrap metal is a potential bullet against Hitler. We would never fling away a bullet. We must never fling away one piece of scrap that can be salvaged. In this matter men and women in the home have a duty as vital as the men and women in the arms works."

With these words Mr. Herbert Morrison, Minister of Supply, underlined the announcement, made last night, that the collection of salvage is to be made **compulsory**. All local authorities with populations of more than 10,000 will be required to arrange efficient systems of collection and disposal. All householders in the areas of these local authorities will have to co-operate in a new nation-wide anti-waste campaign.

Mr. Morrison made his decision following a recommendation by the committee of women M.P.s set up at the end of May under the chairmanship of Miss Megan Lloyd George to advise him on salvage questions. This is its first recommendation to the Minister.

Most urgently needed are waste **paper** and **cardboard**, scrap **metals**, and household **bones**. Other materials such as waste food and rags may be added to the list from time to time.

It is to speed up the collection of these materials by mobilising millions of households and hundreds of local authorities that the new decisions have been taken.

It is proposed to follow the directions to local authorities with an order requiring householders to make these materials available for collection. Details of methods of collection—which will be as simple as possible—will be made known in each district.

TASK FOR ALL

While responsibility for seeing that collection of salvage is properly organised will rest with local councils, provision is to be made for utilising merchants, rag-and-bone men, and voluntary organisations who have already given important help.

Said Mr. Morrison yesterday : " I call for more scrap—as I have called for more arms. I am certain that the whole nation will respond to an appeal which affects everyone equally and which none has good reason to evade. This is a war job for each one of us."

They Gave Up Week-End For The Children

KING TO HIS SER

SHOULD an air raid warn private A.R.P. post at Bu bers of the staff who have b and first-aid personnel woul King and Queen would o implicitly.

The air-raid precautions at the palace provide an example any household can follow with profit. Everything is prepared beforehand and reduced to the simplest and quickest organisation; and everybody, from the King and Queen to the youngest pantry-boy, knows exactly what to do in an emergency.

Every day the deep cellar shelter rooms are inspected and made ready. Fresh water is stored by the little stove for making hot drinks, and there are tins of biscuits and sweets, periodically replaced. Once a week the rooms are thoroughly warmed through, to prevent an accumulating dampness which might cause chills.

QUEEN'S KNITTING

Bring Out Your Pans

By Daily Mail Reporter

The appeal by Lord Beaverbrook, Minister of Aircraft Production, for aluminium kitchenware to help Britain's drive for air supremacy, has "caught on" with women everywhere.

Dozens of them, with bags and suitcases, laden with pans, kettles, shoe-trees, fish-slices, coffee-pots, and every sort of aluminium article, arrived at the Westminster headquarters of the Women's Voluntary Services before it was open yesterday morning.

"In a few hours we were able to fill a huge display window," Mrs Dunbar, one of the W.V.S. helpers, told me.

Very many articles besides pans are made of aluminium. This list may help you when you are "having a look round":

Bathroom fittings, coat hangers, cigarette cases, car mascots, ornaments, hat pegs, vacuum cleaners, egg boilers, hot-plate covers, door handles, name plates, lamp brackets, and even thimbles.

All contributions are being received at local depots of the Women's Voluntary Services. If you don't know the address ask the police.

39   Pots and pans into Spitfires! The scene at WVS HQ in Union Street, July 1940.

40   Girls' Training Corps marches down Union Street. The YMCA is in the background.

Silk Stockings

HOW LONG WILL YOU HAVE ANY TO WEAR!

THERE'S one sure way to make stockings last—give them a quick squeeze-through in Lux after every wearing. Lux dissolves in *lukewarm* water, and hot water, as you know, is ruinous to delicate silk fibres. Rich Lux lather gets out all the dirt. And because you don't have to rub, the elasticity of threads is preserved—stockings don't ladder.

Always *roll* your stockings on and off. And when washing, trust them only to Lux. What a blessing that Lux is the same price and weight as before the war!

LUX

makes silk stockings last

A *LEVER* PRODUCT   2699-180

Britain, Tuesday, January 28, 1941.

Black-Out Tomorrow: 4.35 p.m.

SUMMER-TIME ends at 3 a.m. tomorrow, and from next week the black-out will descend on Britain an hour earlier. The clock goes BACK.

Many offices and warehouses are planning to close earlier, but, even so, workers will have to go home in the black-out.

The departure of B.S.T. is regretted by shopkeepers and business men, but farmers and others who have to start work early in the day welcome the return of G.M.T. Shopkeepers deplore the change (see Page Nine).

Make note of the revised black-out times :

Tonight   5.36*—6.55a.m.†
Tomorrow 4.35†—6.57 a.m.†

* Summer Time
† Winter Time

THE HOME GUARD

42   A fully equipped Home Guard unit on exercise going "over the top".

The activities of 'Dad's Army' can now be relied upon to bring a wry smile to the lips but its establishment arose out of very real fears. When the Germans invaded Holland and Belgium in May 1940 their paratroops played a leading role and Britain also feared a parachute invasion. On May 14 when Anthony Eden appealed for men between 17 and 65 to form anti-paratroop units guarding installations like factories, power stations and railways there was a tremendous response. At first the units were mainly groups of employees protecting their own works premises and they were called Local Defence Volunteers and wore forage caps and armbands as the only evidence of their appointment (43). They were quickly better armed and given proper uniforms with the very real threat of invasion looming, although it is difficult to imagine the John Lewis Shipbuilders unit defending Aberdeen Harbour with their Lewis Gun and rowing boat (54)!

The short-magazine Lee Enfields were soon supplemented by Canadian Ross rifles, and 'Tommy' guns were sent over by the Americans. The Home Guard was now as well armed as Al Capone (45-9)!

The fall of Norway put Aberdeen in the front line and, because of this, Aberdeen Home Guard units were well supplied and well trained. They were certainly better off than the Lancashire battalion whose total armament consisted of six spears! Old soldiers who had served in the First War brought experience of battle to the ranks although few could equal that of Home Guardsman Alex Taylor from Perthshire who had served in the Egyptian Campaign of 1884-5, and the attempt to relieve General Gordon at Khartoum. Invasion exercises gradually welded the Home Guard into a smart and efficient force (41, 44-7) and by the time of the 3rd Birthday Parade of Aberdeen Home Guard on May 16 1943 it was "impressive in numbers, bearing and Equipment", according to the *Press & Journal* (50-2): 3,000 Home Guardsmen took three quarters of an hour to pass the saluting base at the Music Hall in Union Street, where Lord Provost Thomas Mitchell took the salute.

43   The first parade of No 3 company, Local Defence Volunteers, June 7, 1940. Uniform at this stage is limited to forage caps and armbands although a First War veteran sports his denims and a military decoration.

44   Invasion exercise, May 31 1942.

45   Invasion exercise. Note the woman acting as a civilian casualty; the Home Guard Instructor (with armband) carrying a
      sten gun; the others carry the Canadian Ross rifles and a short magazine Lee Enfield (SMLE).

      In this picture from the invasion exercise series, the soldier takes aim with a SMLE. Note the
46   white blackout painting on the street furniture.

47   Home Guardsmen complete with gas capes, respirators and SMLEs.

48 The Home Guard unit at John Lewis Shipbuilders. The Guardsman on the left has a Thomson sub-machine gun, the 'dead' officer a Webley and the others carry Canadian Ross rifles with fixed bayonets.

49 This Home Guard instructor (6th Aberdeen Home Guard) is armed with a sten gun and from his military medal and campaign medals would appear to be a veteran of the First World War.

50 The 3rd Birthday Parade of Aberdeen Home Guard, May 16, 1943.

51

Home Guard on Brithday Parade in
Union street, led by a Warrant
officer (Class II).

52

Again, the Canadian Ross rifle is in
evidence.

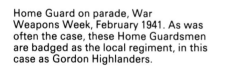

53

Home Guard on parade, War
Weapons Week, February 1941. As was
often the case, these Home Guardsmen
are badged as the local regiment, in this
case as Gordon Highlanders.

54   Just the thing to have Jerry shivering in his shoes! The John Lewis Shipbuilders Home Guard unit defend the harbour with Lewis gun and rowing boat.

THE GORDON HIGHLANDERS

55   The 5/7th Gordon Highlanders in camp in Aberdeenshire, June 1938.

In 1938 the local regiment was preparing for war as the pictures of the mechanised route march through Buchan, the Mearns and Mar indicate (55,6). After the declaration of war there was no lack of volunteers (57,8) and soon new recruits were marching off to dispersal points and basic training. Many found themselves quite quickly in France as part of the 51st Highland Division, itself an integral part of the British Expeditionary Force (61-4). With the invasion of Holland, Belgium and France the men of the 51st were driven back on St. Valery and encircled with no possibility of rescue from the sea. After the initial shock of surrender (65) it became clear that the men of the 51st had fought with gallantry and distrinction. As Eric Linklater wrote two years later:

> ". . . throughout its rearguard action and retreat the Division retained coherence. It remained a Division, and discipline ruled until the very end. It had shown, both on the Saar and the Somme, a finely aggressive spirit and great stubbornness in defence . . . There is no sterner test of discipline than a long rearguard action."

The Division was re-formed and probably its single greatest achievement was the encouragement it gave to the young De Gaulle to fight on from London to free France from the invader.

History repeated itself, alas, in the early months of 1942 when the 2nd Gordons were captured in the fall of Singapore (66).

The re-formed 51st Division broke through Rommel's Afrika Korps at El Alamein at the end of 1943 and swept through Libya, Tripolitania and round to Tunisia. The 6th Gordons featured in landings in French North Africa with distinction. The 51st helped in the capture of Sicily and the 6th Gordons fought at Anzio. The D-Day landings provided the platform for final vengeance. The Gordons were in the front line in the sweep across France, Belgium and Holland (67-70). There was tough fighting in the Caen sector after the landing and Gordons helped in the capture of Le Havre and, fittingly, the liberation of St. Valery. They helped stem the Ardennes counter attack and were first to reach the east bank of the Rhine. Among the first across the Rhine, the Regimental drum — not seen since the surrender at St. Valery — was restored to the Regiment after discovery by American troops (70,1) in Munich outside the library building of the Nazi regime.

Lasting links were now forged between Aberdeen and St. Valery and a monument in granite was made in Aberdeen (73), transported to France and celebrated in many a civic ceremony (74).

56

Aberdeenshire route march (June 1938) and feeding time in camp.

57

"You're in the army now!" Conscripts arrive at the Gordons Barracks, Bridge of Don.

58

Medical examination of conscripts at Bridge of Don.

59   September 9, 1939 and the serious business of war begins.

The 5th Gordon Highlanders deposit their colours for safekeeping at Stoneywood Polo
60   Park. Below, the colours are escorted off.

61   The 5th Gordons leave Bucksburn for the train, October 7, 1939.

62   Gordons on the march in Union Terrace, October 5, bound for the station.

63   Gordons depart with ill concealed contempt for the Führer! (April 17, 1940).

65 An official picture titled "Scots do some shopping in France" (October 16, 1939). Things are still fairly light hearted as the intricacies of French cooking utensils are demonstrated to these soldiers.

64 Surrender at St. Valery. Extreme right, General Fortune, Commander of the 51st Highland Division. Also in the picture, General Rommel and, foreground, General Imler, Commander of the French IX Corps.

66   General Wavell talks to the C.O. of the Gordon Highlanders, Lt. Col. Graham, at Singapore, November 3, 1941. To the right is Lt. Gen. Percival, G.O.C. Malaya. who later surrendered Singapore to the Japanese in a crushing blow to British morale.

Lance Bombardier G. Douglas and Gunner A. Douglas, both from Aberdeen, meet in the Caen sector in
67   1944 for the first time after five years in the Highland Division. An official photograph.

68

Carriers and 6-pounder anti-tank guns of the 1st Battalion Gordon Highlanders move up to battle positions in south west Holland near Loon-op-Zand, October 30, 1944.

69

Men of the 5/7th Gordons snatch some sleep, November 1944.

70

Men of the 5/7th Gordons combing the Reichswald Forest, February 1945

71   Brigadier Sinclair hands Corporal W Sim of the 5/7th Gordons the Regimental Drum captured by the Germans and recovered by the U S 7th Army, Munich June 7 1945.

72

Corporal W Sim beats the Regimental Drum again in a handing over ceremony on Munich's Königplatz, June 7 1945. Behind is the library building of the Nazi Party.

73   The 51st Highland Division granite memorial leaves Aberdeen by road in 1956 for St Valery.

Pipes and drums of the 51st Highland Volunteers grouped around the Division memorial at
74   St Valery in 1969.

AIR FORCES AT DYCE & PETERHEAD

75 Avro Anson of 612 "County of Aberdeen" Squadron Auxiliary Air Force at Dyce, 1938.

Well before the outbreak of war, it was realised that the north east of Scotland had a strategic importance requiring protection with coastal shipping rounding Rattray Head and Kinnaird Head, the fishing fleet based at Aberdeen and the likelihood of establishing a swept channel free from mines six or seven miles offshore.

No 612 (County of Aberdeen) Auxiliary Air Force Squadron was formed at Dyce on June 1 1937 under Squadron Leader Finlay Crerar and it was initially designated an army cooperation unit flying the tough little biplane the Hawker Hector (76,7). The Squadron also had a Hawker Hart trainer and three Avro Tutors (77). In November 1938 the designation was changed from Army Cooperation to General Reconnaissance, and the Squadron received the more sophisticated Avro Anson (75) in July 1939. On August 4 one of the Ansons was instructed to intercept the German airship *Graf Zeppelin* on its celebrated spy flight over the east coast. 612 Squadron moved up to Wick at the end of March 1941.

In July 1941 the first all-Czech Squadron — 310 — formed in Britain as part of the Royal Air Force

scramble arrived at Dyce with their Hurricanes (79,80). From January 1940 No 603 City of Edinburgh Squadron, Auxiliary Air Force, flew the Mark 1 Spitfire from Dyce and, later, the Mark VB (81). No 248 Squadron, Coastal Command, flew early Beaufighters on patrol into the North Sea right up to the Faroes Gap (82). The Luftwaffe tip-and-run raids on Aberdeen, Peterhead and Fraserburgh were undoubtedly discouraged by fighter presence at Aberdeen and Peterhead although the incursions tended to be brief before the invaders fled and it was often difficult to get fighters into the air quickly enough.

No 65 'East India' Squadron was transferred to Scotland in January 1945 to provide fighter escort for the strike wings of Coastal Command operating along the Norwegian coast. The Squadron was based at Peterhead and saw many bloody and bitter battles against the Luftwaffe who fought a spirited rearguard action (84,5).

The City of Aberdeen Squadron, 612, was re-formed in 1946, and flew as an Auxiliary Air Force Squadron from Dyce again from November of that year.

76　No 612 Squadron was formed at Dyce as an army co-operation unit on June 1, 1937 and received Hawker Hectors. In this picture, the aircraft is making a low level pass to pick up a message with its retractable hook. Redesignated a general reconnaissance squadron in November, 1938, it then received Avro Ansons.

　　On the grass at Dyce in 1938, the first three aricraft are Hawker Hectors, the fourth is a Hawker Hart trainer and the
77　last three are Avro Tutors.

78   Prince Bernhard of the Netherlands visits the RAF station at Dyce, January 25, 1941.

79   Pictured at Dyce, pilots of the first all Czech squadron (No 310) to be formed in Britain as part of the Royal Air Force scramble.

80   Hurricanes of No 310 Czech Squadron at Dyce, October 24, 1941. The squadron was based at Dyce July 20 — December 24, 1941, before moving south to Cornwall.

Mk VB Spitfire of No 603 "City of Edinburgh" Squadron, Auxiliary Air Force, at Dyce February 19, 1942. During the Battle of Britain, No 603 Squadron achieved the third highest score with 98 enemy aircraft destroyed and, on October 16, 1939 a Spitfire from 603 had shot down the first bomber to be destroyed over Britain in the War in an air battle over the
81   Firth of Forth.

82   An early Beaufighter VIc with horizontal tailplane of No 248 Squadron Coastal Command at Dyce, April 1942. The squadron was engaged in long range fighter patrols over the North Sea. Beneath the nose can be seen the muzzles of the four 20 mm cannon which, along with the six 303 in machine guns in the outer wings, made for a formidable strike capacity.

83   Mosquito crash on house at Dyce, August 1943.

84   Mustang IVs of No 65 "East India" Squadron at Peterhead with long range auxiliary fuel tanks fitted beneath the wings. These fuel tanks were made of bonded paper for lightness.

85   Mustang IVs of No 65 "East India" Squadron at Peterhead, April 20, 1945. The squadron was transferred to Scotland in January 1945 to provide fighter escort for the strike wings of Coastal Command operating along the Nortwegian coast, where many bitterly fought actions against the Luftwaffe Rearguard were experienced.

86   A Wellington aircraft crashed on landing at Dyce on May 16 1945, wrecking a goods train in Dyce railway station. Two airmen were killed.

87   Mustang III of No 65 "East India" Squadron. The aircraft is fitted with a Malcolm Hood, a cockpit canopy designed by the British to alleviate the poor visibility inherent in the original American design. The Mustang III was equipped with a Packard-built Rolls-Royce Merlin engine. Pictured at Peterhead RAF Station, April 20, 1945.

H M S ABERDEEN & H M S SCYLLA

Launched at Devonport in January 1936, H M S *Aberdeen* was a Grimsby Class escort sloop, displacing 990 tons with a maximum speed of around 16. 5. knots. She was originally designed to carry a main armament of four 4 in. guns but in fact carried only two in peacetime so as to provide extra accommodation whilst attached to the flagship, Mediterranean Fleet.

During the War her armament was increased and she also carried depth charges. By 1943-44 *Aberdeen* and her sister ship H M S *Fleetwood* were split off into a class of their own.

Aberdeen was decommissioned at the end of the War and on December 16 1948 she was sold for scrap and broken up at Hayle in January 1949. H M S *Fleetwood* was disarmed and refitted as a Radar Experimental Ship until 1959 when, she too, was sold for scrap.

HMS *Scylla* was launched at Scott's Shipbuilding & Engineering yard in July 1940 and was the eighth of 16 cruisers comprising the Dido Class. *Scylla* and her sister ship H M S *Charybis* were completed with extemporised armament of eight 4½ in., eight 2-pounder anti-aircraft and eight 20 mm. anti-aircraft guns — the five 5.25 in. guns these ships were designed to carry were not available during construction. *Scylla's* A/A armament was later enhanced by the replacement of her 2 pounders with 40 mm. weapons.

In June 1942 H M S *Scylla* was formally adopted by the City and people of Aberdeen. In a ceremony aboard the ship Lord Provost Mitchell handed over a silver cigar box from the City to the officers and a ship's Bible to the company from the Sunday school children of the West Church of St. Nicholas. The *P & J* correspondent noted, "With a maternal affection we shall share the triumphs and anxieties of the gay and gallant band of adventurous young men who man her."

Addressing the 500-strong company after a march past, Lord Provost Mitchell referred to the fact that Aberdonians had raised £3,600,000 (as against a target of £2,700,000) in Warship Week Appeal.

The war record of H M S *Scylla* was distinguished and one of which both her crew and the people of Aberdeen could be proud. She was the flagship for the famous Russian convoy PQ18 which left Loch Ewe on September 2 1942. This heavily defended convoy suffered continued attacks from enemy aircraft and U-boats; there were over a hundred attacks by torpedo bombers and slightly fewer than that by high-level and dive-bombers. Despite these concerted attacks only 13 ships were lost and *Scylla* was responsible for downing many enemy aircraft and for eventually leading the convoy into harbour at Dvina. She sailed as an A/A cruiser with convoy JW 53 in February 1943 and, largely thanks to efficient anti-aircraft protection, that convoy reached Murmansk safely.

After the Russian convoys she joined the Home Fleet and during the D-Day landings was the flagship for the Eastern Bombardment Force in the British sector. On June 23 1944 she was mined sustaining severe underwater damage. She was not repaired and was eventually sold for scrap and broken up at Barrow.

H.M.S. "Aberdeen".

H.M.S. "Scylla" in the Clyde.

91   Aberdeen civic visit to HMS "Scylla" June 7, 1942. Lord Provost Tom Mitchell salutes as a Royal Marine band plays.

92   Ratings crowd the deck on the occasion of the offficial visit to H.M.S. Scylla.

INDUSTRY AT WAR

93   Coastal command pilots visit the Wilson Enginnering Works, May 1943. Left, is F.O. G.H. Scott of Aberdeen and, right, F.O. A.R.A. Hunt, D.F.C.

Perhaps the single most dramatic feature of industry during the Second World War was the mobilisation of women in the war effort. Throughout Britain over 7½ million women were mobilised — either in the factories or auxiliary services. As Lewis observes in *A Peoples War,* "Probably the most important change the war brought to women was the change in their picture of themselves and of their potential."

At the end of 1941, amid much controversy, there was the order for conscription of unmarried women aged 19-20. There was the choice between the women's services, civil defence or industry. Speaking at Abereden on April 30 1943, Mr. Bevin announced that 90 % of single women between the ages of 18 and 40 were in industry or the services. Government training centres were set up for women going into industry (113) with surprising results for the planners. Sir Emrys Jones a wartime Cultivation Officer, observed: "They were the most trainable human beings I have ever had".

Women tackled a previously unheard of range of jobs with consumate success (93, 109, 110) and there was

regular flow of Governmental or Royal visitors to boost morale and production (95, 110, 111).

The fishing industry prospered during the war and queues for fish were usually long as it was not rationed. Lord Woolton, Minister of Food, visited Aberdeen in 1943 (95) to encourage the industry by way of a change from Woolton Pie (a much promoted concoction of potatoes, swedes and carrots).

The Hall Russell shipyards turned out a seemingly endless stream of vessels for the Navy (97-108) — frigates, corvettes, tugs, travelers and survey vessels — and, in return became a Luftwaffe target (96). In the raid of July 12 1940 a lone bomber killed workers at their lunch break before being brought down itself on the new ice rink at South Anderson Drive.

Prisoners of war were put to work either on farms or on the roads. The Monymusk POW camp was in Deer Park, opposite Monymusk School, and there were both Italians and Germans held there (114—16.) By all accounts, relations with the local community were remarkably good and many lifetime links were forged.

95   Aberdeen Harbour was barricaded and defended.

Lord Woolton, Minister of Food, visits Aberdeen Fish Market, June 21, 1943. Fish queues were usually long as fish was
94   not rationed during the War.

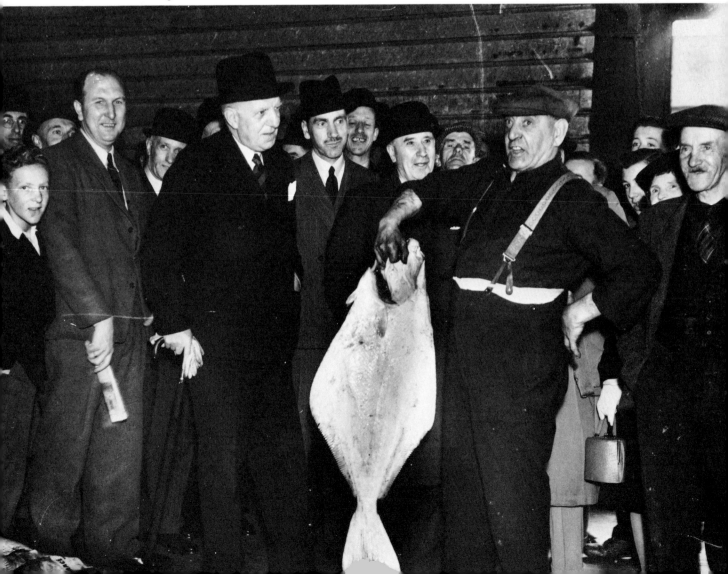

The Hall Russell Shipyard was a Luftwaffe target. This picture shows damage inflicted after a 1941 raid.

(1)
TRANSPORT FERRY CONSTRUCTION
Beam view of Transport Ferry.
In the foreground are frigates
under construction.

Construction photographs showing progress on a transport ferry.

A general view of the Hall Russell yard in 1940.

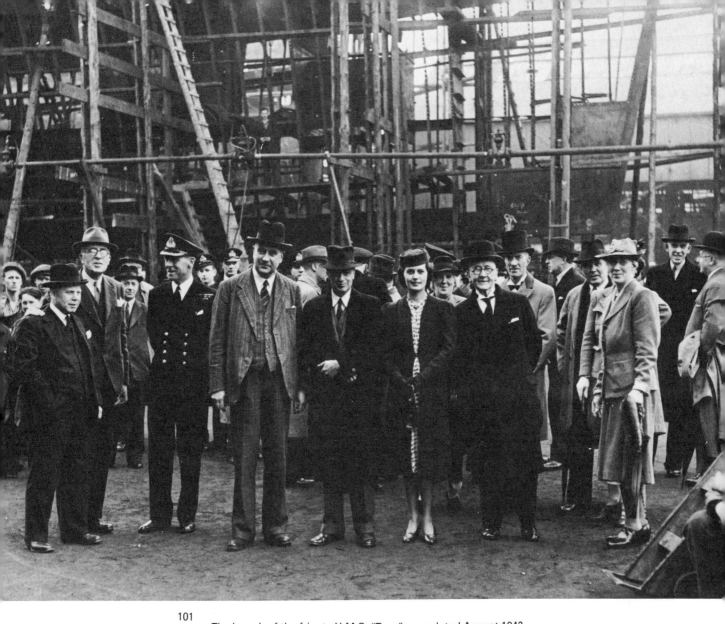

101

102 The launch of the frigate H.M.S. "Tees", completed August 1943.

103

Admiralty Trawler "Sir Kay", completed February, 1943.

104

Admiralty Trawler "Sir Lamorak", completed March, 1943.

105

H.M. Frigate "Tees", completed August, 1943.

106

H.M. Frigate "Helford", completed June 1943.

107

H.M. Tug "Capable".

108

H.M. Frigate "Bigbury Bay", begun May 1944 and completed July 1945.

109   Aberdeen Munitions Factory. Ammunition Girls, April 1941.

110   The Duchess of Gloucester visits Aberdeen Munitions Factory, October 29, 1942.

111   Bob Boothby, MP, Parliamentary Secretary to the Ministry of Food, eats in the women's canteen at Broadford Works, September 1940.

112   Shipyard workers at Hall Russell & Co. hold a Christmas Service in the Boilermakers' Shop, December 24, 1943.

113   Women train as motor mechanics at a Government Emergency Training Centre, November 1942.

114　German prisoners-of-war from the Monymusk Camp.

115　POWs working on the roads — believed to be in the Seaton Park area.

116　Fritz is put to work on the roads — a common use for POWs.

THE BOMBING

118 The Royal Observer Corps Headquarters at Woolmarhill. Personnel are wearing police armbands — probably surplus-endorsed "Observer Corps".

Aberdeen was the most frequently bombed City in Scotland with no less than 34 attacks and 178 people killed. Most of the attacks were sudden, brief affairs known as 'tip-and-run' raids made by an individual or a small number of planes — often unloading bombs meant for coastal shipping before flying back to base in Norway or Denmark.

Members of the Royal Observer Corps would keep watch for these raiders and telephone information to Headquarters in the operations room at Woolmanhill (118). After an isolated minor attack in January 1940, the raids started in late June. On June 26 1940 a bungalow at Nigg was destroyed and on July 1 bombs fell at the Beach Promenade (124) and on Victoria Road School (125). July 12 saw the most serious attack yet when a solitary Heinkel III came in over the north of the City dropping bombs in King Street, Marischal Street and on the Hall Russell Yard at Footdee (129). Bombs scored a direct hit on the boiler house and apprentices at lunch were killed. Four men were killed at the doorway of the Neptune Bar and the bomber headed away towards Rosemount. At that point it was intercepted by Spitfires scrambled from Dyce and somewhere over Duthie Park it was mortally damaged. The plane went low over

houses at Ruthrieston and eventually crashed on the site of the new ice rink at South Anderson Drive (127,8) A total of 34 people were killed. On August 28 a bomb was dropped on Forbesfield Road (159) and the next day Oscar Road in Torry was bombed.

A raid in November 1940 inflicted serious damage at Torry (130-33). In a spectacular blaze, the Palace Hotel on Union Street was burned down following a raid on October 31 1941 (137, 141). On February 13 1942 the premises of Ogston & Tennant in Loch Street were hit by incendiaries and high explosives. Mc Brides Bar across the road was also hit and patrons buried in the debris. In all, 17 people were killed (138, 39). On the night of August 7 1942 the South Market Street area was badly hit (146-8). A nurse and two members of a rescue squad lost their lives while searching the debris for victims. Mrs Mary Park, Mr James Dow and Mr James Watt were trapped by a fall of masonry bringing the toll for the night to 7 killed.

The worst raid of the war was that on the night of April 21 1943 (see Introduction). In a pre-planned air raid 25 Dorniers swept in from the north of the City and 98 people were killed and there was extensive damage to the north of the City (149-160).

119   Wartime Aberdeen in May 1942 as Luftwaffe pilots would have seen it.

120   Observer Corps Bucksburn Post, February 1940.

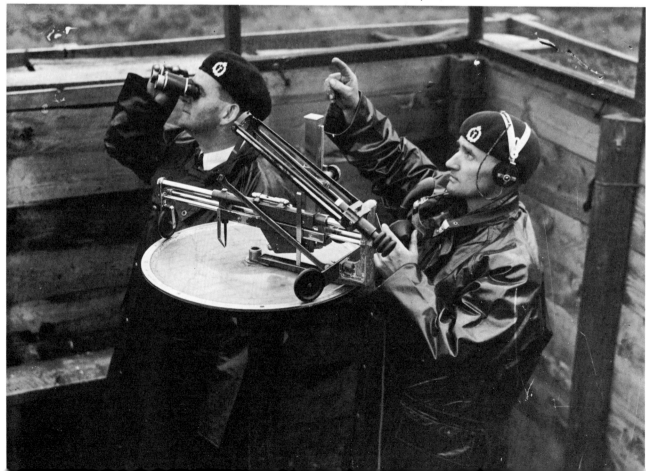

121 Barrage balloon under tow in Aberdeen Harbour.

WOMEN WANTED
to take over the
BALLOON BARRAGE

The nightmare of Nazi airmen is Britain's balloon barrage. That's why it is one of the most important jobs in the country to keep those silver fish flying! And the WAAF have proved they can take over this important front-line job from the RAF!

It's a fine, healthy life for women who are fit and strong and fond of the open air. You must be 5' 1" or over, and aged between 17½ and 43. After a short training course, you will be posted to a balloon site. Sites are usually in or near a town. There you will live and work in a small community of about a dozen or so. When fully trained your minimum pay is 3/- a day *and all found.*

In addition to balloon operation, there are many other interesting trades open now in the WAAF. Every woman not doing vital work is asked to volunteer.

A Serviceman's wife does NOT lose her allowance on joining up, and she IS granted her leave to coincide with her husband's leave, subject only to urgent Service considerations.

Go to a Recruiting Centre* or Employment Exchange for fuller information. If you are in work, *they* will find out whether you can be spared from it. If you cannot go at once, send in the coupon.

When this girl joined the WAAF six months ago, to become a balloon operator, she was badly under weight. Now she's back to normal. " You can tell them from me, it's a grand life!" she says.

*Single girls born between January 1st, 1918, and June 30th, 1922, come under the National Service Act and *must* go to the Employment Exchange, *not* a Recruiting Centre.

WAAF

297 Oxford Street, London, W.1   3010   *AR 10*

Please send me full information about the trade of Balloon Operator in the WAAF.

Mrs. ⎱
Miss ⎰   Cross out " Mrs." or " Miss "

Address _____

122 Later in the war, women took over the operation of the balloon barrage, previously considered too arduous for them.

123   An early victim of the bombing. The Grimsby trawler "Etruria" was bombed off Aberdeen by Nazi planes, December 18, 1939.

124   Bomb damage to Aberdeen Beach Promenade, July 1, 1940.

125   Victoria Road School, Torry, July I, 1940.

126   Crowds gather outside Victoria Road School to survey one of the first victims of bomb damage.

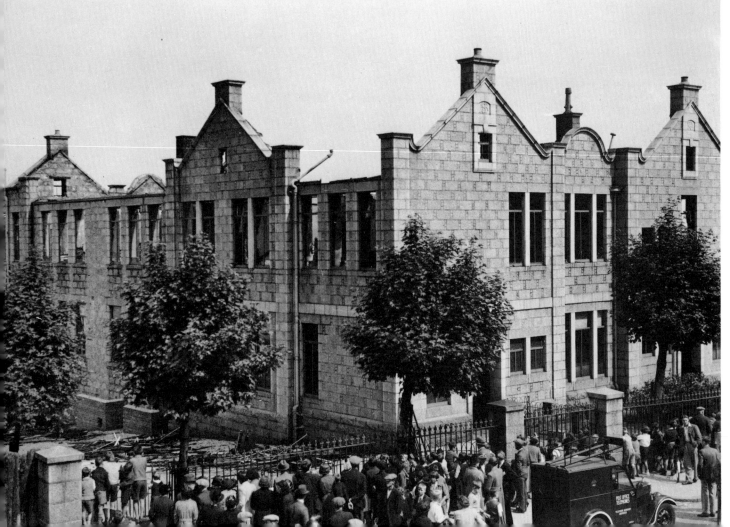

Pursuing Spitfires shot down a Heinkel III which then crashed into Aberdeen's new South Anderson Drive Ice Rink, July 12, 1940 at lunchtime after an attack on the city.

128   The wreck of the Nazi bomber.

Damage at Urquhart Road and a granite yard, July 12, 1940.

130   Bomb damage at 55 Wellington Road, November 4, 1940.

131   Survivors of the attack at Wellington Road.

Personal possessions are salvaged from
Wellington Road.

133

Survivors take refuge in a temporary rest
centre in Torry.

134   Workmen struggle to extricate a cleansing department lorry from debris after the depot in Poynerhook Road was seriously damaged on August 6, 1941.

135   Bomb damage at Menzies Road, August 8, 1941.

136   Possessions are salvaged from Menzies Road.

137   The Palace Hotel burns on the night of October 31, 1941.

138   McBrides Bar, Loch Street, February 13, 1942.

139   The Loch Street raid.

141   The ruins of the Palace Hotel at the corner of Bridge Street and Union Street (now the site of the C & A Department Store).

142   Bomb damage in the Froghall area, April 21, 1943.

143 Damage to Porthill Church in the Gallowgate, April 25, 1942.

144   King Street was pockmarked by bombs on the night of April 25, 1942.

146   Damage in the South Market Street area, August 7, 1942.

147   South Market Street.

148   Salvage in the aftermath of the South Market Street raid.

149 Bomb damage in Cattofield, April 21, 1943.

150 Damage was widespread in Cattofield.

151 This Cattofield air raid shelter suffered a direct hit.

152   This is how the Berlin **Illustrierte Zeitung** reported the April 1943 raid on Aberdeen — the city's worst raid of the war.

153

Bomb damage near Causewayend Church, April 21, 1943.

154   Causewayend Church, April 21, 1943.

Killed by enemy
action 21st April
19   43

Kathleen A.S. Mitche
aged 5 years. Jun
L. Porter aged 9 year
Ernest M. Wallac
aged 10 years. Rober
Reid aged 10 year
John M. Moir age
9 years. Erected b
scholars and staf

155   A sad memorial at Sunnybank Primary to yo
       pupils who died in the April 21 attack.

156   Bomb craters and wrecked tombstones in
       St Peter's Cemetery.

The aftermath of the April 21 raid and the funeral cortege for
Bedford Road the Cattofield victims winds its way down Seaforth
158   Road en route to Trinity Cemetery.

157   Trinity Cemetery and the burial of the
       unidentified victims of the April 21 raid.

159   Bomb damage at Forbesfield Road, Mrs. Shirreffs House, August 29, 1940.
This was the first — and one of the very few — pictures of bomb damage in Aberdeen published during the war.

160   Industrial damage at Richards Mill, Broadford Works, April 1943.

PETERHEAD & FRASERBURGH

161   The Duke of Kent speaks to members of the crew of Fraserburgh Lifeboat, July 14, 1939. Making the presentations (right) is Provost Thompson.

In terms of their size, the fishing ports of Peterhead and Fraserburgh suffered seriously from air attack. Situated on that knuckle of land jutting out into the North Sea, they were sitting targets for the Luftwaffe planes detailed to attack shipping rounding Kinnaird and Rattray Heads. There was also the naval base at Peterhead which was a prime target.

The area was known as 'Hellfire Corner' and Fraserburgh was dubbed 'Little London': 87 bombs were dropped on the town, killing 49 and injuring 249. Fifty-nine houses and 24 other buildings were completely destroyed and 1296 houses damaged. The town suffered 23 raids, the worst of which was on the night of November 5 1940. A fire started in Benzie & Miller's department store and a German bomber returning to base with unused bombs aboard unleashed its deadly cargo.

Peterhead was the recipient of 78 bombs, killing 38 people and injuring 44. Fifty-eight houses were destroyed and 1138 damaged (164-75).

In December 1943, Sir Stafford Cripps, Minister of Aircraft Production, visited the aircraft factory at Fraserburgh as part of his tireless round of morale boosting visits (177, 78).

162   The Duke of Kent watching the unloading of herring at Peterhead. To the Duke's left is Provost Schultze.

163   On board the motor drifter "Faithful" at Fraserburgh Harbour. On the Duke's right is Skipper William Whyte.

164   Bomb damage to Peterhead Academy, July 20, 1940.

165   Bomb damage, Peterhead, August 10, 1941.

166   Searching the rubble at Peterhead.

167

Houses collapsed like a deck of cards.

168   Peterhead, September 5, 1941.

169   Peterhead, September 29, 1940.

170   Searching the rubble after the September 29, 1940 raid on Peterhead.

171   Bringing out the dead

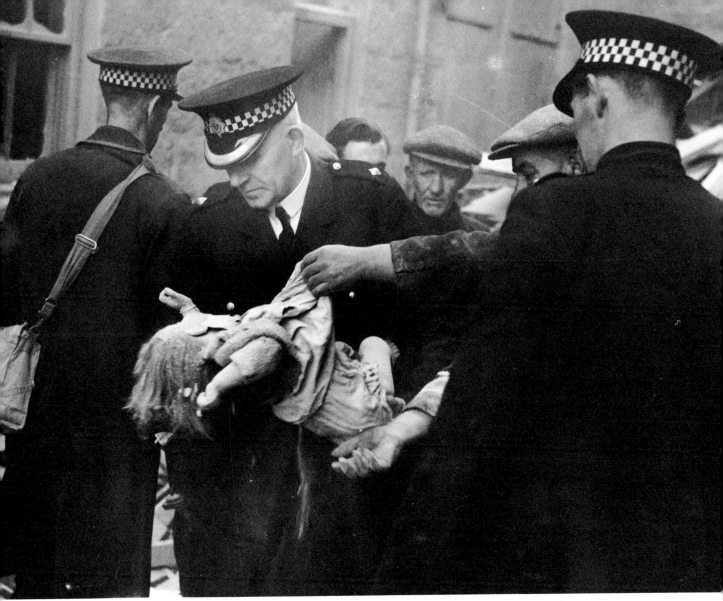

172   A young survivor at Peterhead, September 29, 1940.

173   Bread is sold in the streets in the aftermath of the raid.

174

Survivors of an August 1941 raid on Peterhead clutch salvaged possessions. Mrs Cooke (centre of group) just managed to reach the shelter as the bomb burst.

175

Peterhead bomb damage, October 1941.

176

Residents salvage furniture from devastated houses in the Harbour Street/Cross Street area of Fraserburgh, February 1943.

177   Sir Stafford Cripps, Minister of Aircraft Production, addresses workers at the aircraft factory in Fraserburgh.

178   Sir Stafford Cripp tours the Fraserburgh Factory, December 13, 1943.

179   This 'home made' Peterhead air raid shelter withstood an August 1941 air raid.

NO MORE BANANAS FOR BRITAIN

By Daily Mail Reporter

BANANAS will be banned from Britain as from the end of December.

The reason? They are too big.

An official of the Ministry of Food said yesterday: " Bananas are a bulky cargo compared with other food. Oranges, for instance, have far greater vitamin value than bananas—and occupy far less space.

" We want to use ships for more important cargoes than bananas."

The great Banana Ban—which puts grim truth in the words of the old song. " Yes, we have no Bananas "—burst like a bombshell in Covent Garden.

An official of the Colonial Office walked into the London offices of the biggest banana importers in the world and said: " I am sorry, but no more licences for the importation of bananas will be issued."

The prohibition will throw over a thousand men out of work in this country, and seriously affect the economic position of Jamaica, whose banana trade represents over half of the island's total exports.

Messrs. Elders and Fyffes, the importers, are protesting to the Government.

" We thought it might be because the Government required our ships," an official said, " but we were informed that there is no shortage of ships.

" While bananas are just commercial to us, they are a real, nourishing, honest-to-goodness food for women and children."

Before the war this country consumed 45,000,000 bananas a week, but war-time restrictions have reduced that by about half. In 1938 Jamaica shipped us £2,400,000 worth.

THE HOME FRONT

180   The Music Hall decorated for Salute the Soldier Week, May 1944.

There was much emphasis on morale boosting parades (182-4), fundraising (181) and the exercise of general economies.

The British Restaurants were introduced, organised by the local authority and staffed by the WVS, offering square meals for under a shilling a head (186, 87). There was much demand for their services and not only were meals served at the restaurants at Powis, Justice Street, Oscar Road (Torry), Rubislaw, Castlehill and Middlefield, but meals were sent to outlying farms during the 'hairst', to the fish market for Sunday landings and to works canteens. Not all recipients were grateful. The managing director of Spark's of Aberdeen wrote to Miss MacAulay, the Supervisor of Communal Feeding: "This is most unsatisfactory and we would advise that the fish pie served for last nights tea was bad and having a decided metalic (sic) flavour".

On November 2 1942 Drumtochty Castle was opened by King Haakon as a school for refugee Norwegian children (195-7). The children came from Spitsbergen,

the Lofoten Islands and Norway itself and some 60 were accommodated at the Castle. The opening ceremony was colourful with teachers and children in national dress although the children surprised locals with a perfect rendering of 'Auld Lang Syne'!

More than 100,000 farm workers left the land before 1940 to join the forces and by 1944, 80,000 women had joined the Women's Land Army. There was a training school at Craibstone Farm which trained 60 girls a month. After their training they marched off in their smart uniform of coduroy breeches, leggings, boots and green jumper topped off with a khaki broad-rimmed hat (198).

In the interests of economy Stay at Home Holidays were widely promoted and there were organised activities, dances and demonstrations at Hazlehead during Trades Week (199-204). In 1944 there was an impressive march past by 130 girls of the Women's Timber Corps based in camps in the forests of Aberdeen, Kincardine, Banff and Moray (back cover).

181   A captured Junkers 88 on view at Marischal College, February 1941.

182   The Home Guard march down Union Street in full battledress during Salute the Soldier Week, May 27—June 3, 1944.

183   A section of the crowd at the corner of Dee Street and Union Street during Salute the Soldier Week.

184

The parade in Union Street.

MINISTRY OF FOOD

YOUR NEW 'RATION BOOK'

HOW TO REGISTER WITH THE SHOPS

The new Ration Books are now being distributed. As soon as you receive your new Book you must fill in the particulars as explained below, and then take the Book to the shops for fresh Registration. It has been found possible to allow *immediate* Registration, and the sooner you register the better. This is what to do :—

1 On the pages of coupons for Rationed Foods (Meat, Bacon, Butter and Sugar) you must fill in your name and address (BLOCK LETTERS) in the space provided in the centre of each page.

2 At the foot of these pages are spaces marked 'Counterfoil'. Here you must write your name and address, the date, and the name and address of the shop where you wish to buy the particular food during the six months' period beginning July 8th.

3 Inside the front cover of your Ration Book you must write the names and addresses of the shops.

4 As soon as you have done this, take the Book to each of the shops with whom you intend to register, so that they may cut out their counterfoils.

EVERYONE MUST REGISTER FOR THE NEW PERIOD

The Ministry of Food is responsible both for the supply and quality of rationed foods. No retailer is, therefore, in a better position than another to secure supplies of rationed foods, nor can one retailer promise to provide a better quality than another.

186   A British Restaurant van at Ruthrieston offers two "coarses" (sic.) for 9d and three for 11d, March

187   The first three diners are served at the British Restaurant at Powis Community Centre, March 9,

189 Munros Transport, Mounthooly, converted this petrol driven lorry to run on coal gas.

COAL

Use Coal carefully
Be glad of any Coal
Don't worry about the kind
Your merchant will supply
the best he can

Ask your supplier for FREE booklets on how to save coal and coke and watch these hints.

NEVER WASTE HOT WATER
NEVER USE SOOTY PANS
NEVER FORCE THE BOILER

ISSUED BY THE MINES DEPARTMENT

Your kitchen range must burn less this winter !

Get to know it better. Persuade it to do more — for less ! Every scuttle saved means more for the factories, to swell the output of weapons — to finish the job.

ECONOMISE IN EVERY WAY YOU CAN

Here are some examples:

Have a fire in one room only—breakfast in the kitchen	Wrap up hot water pipes and tanks to retain heat
Never use your oven for a single dish	Waste occurs when dampers are open unnecessarily
Use less hot water for baths and washing up	Sift and use all cinders, and use coal dust for banking

Call at your Coal Office or Gas or Electricity Showroom for advice and leaflets on how to economise.

Save FUEL for the factories

All Fuels are equally important

COAL · COKE · GAS · ELECTRICITY · FUEL OIL · PARAFFIN

ISSUED BY THE MINES DEPARTMENT

191 King George and Queen Elizabeth in Aberdeen March 10, 1941.

192 Queen Elizabeth visits the naval hospital at Kingseat, March 1, 1940 accompanied by Lord Provost Mitchell and a Surgeon Rear-Admiral.

193   October 1944 saw the first solo engagement for the young Princess Elizabeth in Aberdeen. Here she inspects Sea Rangers at the opening of the Sailors' Home.

194   Princess Elizabeth at Foresterhill Hospital with war wounded, October 3, 1944.

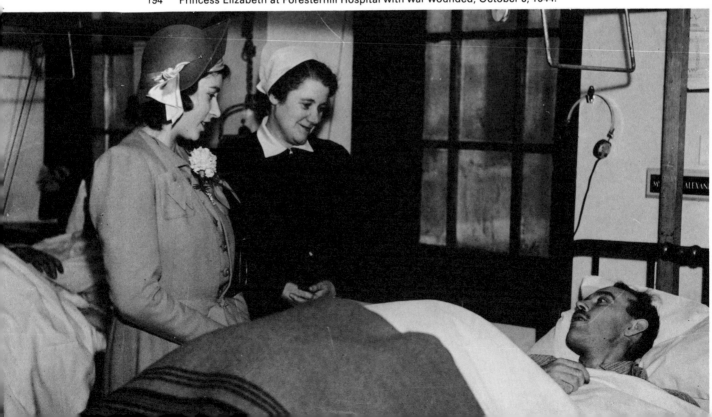

195　　Nine Aberdeen evacuees ('Seavacs') on the eve of their departure for South Africa. Left to right: Doris Adams, David Forbes, Ewen Forbes, Norma Keatings, Audrey Brebner, Anthony Forbes, Dennis Clifford, George Angus, Lena Gentle.

196　King Haakon, wearing the uniform of a Norwegian Admiral of the Fleet, at Drumtochty Castle, Aberdeenshire, November 2, 1942.

197　The Norwegian flag is raised at Drumtochty Castle as youngsters look on.

198　A force to be reckoned with! Women's Land Army girls on parade during War Weapons Week, February 1941.

199   A large crowd watches an open air show at Hazelhead Park during Trades

142. This was mounted as part of the Stay at Home Holiday campaign.

200   Stay at Home Holiday games, July 1942.

201   A shortage of men for these dances. Stay at Home Holidays, July 1944.

202   A picnic in the park, July 1944.

203   Scottish Country Dancing, Hazelhead Park, July 1942.

204   Beautiful Baby Contest in the rain, July 1944

Women's Latest in Crime

SILK STOCKING SNATCHING

WHEN the Government cut down the shops' supplies of silk stockings they started a new crime wave among women, according to police officials in Glasgow.

Nine women were charged there with stealing silk stockings from stores. One was a professional dancer, another a telephone operator.

Eight of them, ranging in age from 17 to 49, admitted taking the stockings and were fined. The ninth pleaded not guilty and was remanded.

Half-day Thefts

Wednesday and Saturday half-holidays, said the police, were the most popular times for the offences.

The sentences of the court were :

Emily Breen, aged 21, took 2 pairs, fined £2 ; Katherine Murray Stevens, aged 17, 1 pair and other articles, £3 ; Margaret Johnson or Main, aged 43, 1 pair, £2.

Fines of £2, with the option of 20 days' imprisonment, were imposed on Violet Palethorpe or Alston, aged 49, 7 pairs ; Elizabeth Connolly, aged 30, 2 pairs ; Sarah McCallum or Ross, aged 39, 1 pair ; Jessie Milne or Aitken, aged 44, 1 pair ; and Alexandra Dickson, aged 18, 2 pairs.

206 June 1944 and the first news of the Normandy landings draws a crowd.

PROVOST CAME TO TOWN

From Aberdeen to Honour Smuts

By Daily Mail Reporter

FIELD-MARSHAL SMUTS yesterday became a Freeman of Aberdeen—in a London hotel.

Probably no such ceremony has before had such a private, happy, family air. Twenty-six chairs had been speculatively arranged for the audience. Only ten were used.

Aberdeen had had to do a scramble to get the casket and prepare the necessary formalities, but as Lord Provost Mitchell said "Aberdonians never get stuck," and Field-Marshal Smuts now possesses a splendid silver box, with the arms of "the ancient City and Royal Burgh" on the lid, and an inscription commemorating the event.

The Lord Provost, fine Scottish blend of dignity and cordiality, brought all the friendliness of the North into play when he said to the field-marshal, "I hope that when you take a cigar it will be out of this box."

Baffled by Light

The box pleased the field-marshal a good deal. He handled it as a great man does a nice piece of work before passing it to son and aide-de-camp Captain Smuts for safe keeping.

When the Lord Provost presented the memento he tried to read the inscription, but the play of light on the incised letters baffled him. The field-marshal took the box over and tried to assist.

Photographers' flashlights frustrated him, too. "Stop that a minute," he said to the cameramen who couldn't help getting close-ups in the tiny room.

All over in less than half an hour, the affair was a model for our public ceremonies. Aberdeen came to London, in the persons of Lord Provost Mitchell, the town clerk, Mr. G. S. Fraser, and the town sergeant, Mr. J. Skene, because the field-marshal could not get up north.

The field-marshal said graceful words of thanks to Aberdeen.

And he said this too:

"You have referred to my services. I need only say this: That I am privileged to have the opportunity once more in my lifetime to take part in a struggle on behalf of human liberty.

"This is my third war, as you know—all three wars of liberty. I have always been on the same side. I have always fought for the same issue, and one hopes that at last this struggle will be the finale, that this war, which exceeds all other wars in human history in its size and extent and ferocity, will be the last which we shall be called upon to wage, at least for a very long time."

'SOLDIER OF FREEDOM'

How the **Daily Mail** reported Field-Marshal Smuts becoming a Freeman of Aberdeen, October 31 1942.

VICTORY!

208   The Aberdeen Journals offices in Broad Street decked out for victory celebrations.

The tide turned in June 1944 with the news of the Normandy landings (206).

The victory celebrations of the summer of 1945 were as enthusiastically embraced by Aberdonians as by all the other long suffering citizens of the country with parades, bonfires and homes and places of work decorated (208—221).

Britain's last air raid warning was sounded simultaneously in Aberdeen and Montrose at 5.20 p.m. on Monday, April 30 1945. The national air raid warning system was discontinued from midday on May 2nd (223). Blackout and lighting restrictions were also abolished — except within five miles of the North Sea coast, lest lurking U-boats unaware of the cessation of hostilities still be on the prowl.

In July and August 1945 the captured U-boat U-776 made a tour of ports on the East coast. She arrived at Aberdeen Harbour on August 6. There was an hour-long queue at Trinity Quay and 3,790 people visited her in the two days she was there (228).

Prisoners of war started to return home — some like Corporal W. Gray with friends acquired in captivity (222: see Introduction).

The 1945—46 football season was an enormous morale booster for the whole of Aberdeen. A capacity crowd packed the Queen's Park Football Club's Hampden Park groud to watch Aberdeen and Rangers do battle in the Scottish Southern League Cup Final in May 1946 (regarded as the first Scottish League Cup Final). The trophy itself who later used for the Victory Cup Final. Aberdeen von 3—2 (scorers Baird, Williams and Taylor).

209   Queueing for fruit at Peglers in Union Street, May 11, 1946. The war may be won but the queues will go on for some time.

Lord Provost Tom Mitchell takes the salute at the Music Hall during the Victory parade of
May 13, 1941. With him are Admiral Sir Lionel Wells, Wing Commander Campbell, Col, I.C. Cameron,
210   Chief Con. McConnach and Mr J.C. Duffus, A.R.P. Controller.

211   Crowds in Union Street, May 13, 1945

212   Crowds gather for VJ Day celebrations, August 15, 1945.

Arriving at the Church of St. Nicholas for the VJ Day Sunday service, August 19, 1945. Lord Provost Tom Mitchell leads civic dignitaries into church (below)

213

214

215   Crowds in Castle Street, August 19, 1945. The Lord Provost surveys the scene.

216   Wrens on parade, VJ Day Sunday parade.

217   The VJ Sunday Parade.

218   Celebrations in the streets August 15, 1945

219   The flags come out for VJ Day.

220   A sea of happy faces on VJ Night.

221   VJ Night and there were bonfires in the streets.

222   August 1945 and Cpl. W. Gray of the 2nd Gordon Highlanders arrives back from a Japanese POW camp with Donald Duck, his wartime campanion. His mother and sister look on.

223   No more need for this rooftop air raid warning siren

224

225   In August 1945 the barricades around Aberdeen Harbour were removed opening up the port again.

226   Demolition of the anti-tank defences on Aberdeen promenade, April 1946.

227

Norwegian fishing boats are 'repatriated'. They are seen here being loaded aboard tank landing craft for transport to Norway.

228   A type VIIc U-Boat — U-776 — in Aberdeen Harbour, August 7, 1945. On the lower gun platform is a 37 mm anti-aircraft gun with a further two twin 20 mm cannon mounted either side of the conning tower. The periscopic Schnorkel is raised to full extension.

229   The 1945/46 football season saw the first Scottish League Cup Final. In the final, Aberdeen met Rangers at Hampden Park. Here Frank Dunlop (left) of Aberdeen and 'Tiger' Shaw of Rangers lead their teams onto the field.

230   Archie Baird (centre) heads Aberdeen's first goal.

231 Aberdeen's winning goal by Taylor. The final scoreline was 3—2.

232 S.F.A. President David Gray presents the League Cup (later Victory Cup) to Aberdeen skipper, Frank Dunlop.

233 A capacity crowd watched Aberdeen beat Rangers.

234 The victorious homecoming. The Aberdeen team arrive at the joint station.

235   Nothing but happy faces at last as these Aberdonians freed from the pressures of war have the additional pleasure
       of awaiting the return of their team with the League Cup.

THE ABERDEEN VICTORIA CROSS

236 Flying officer John A. Cruickshank, V. C. (official Photograph, 1944)

An Aberdonian was responsible for one of the most courageous acts of World War II. John Alexander Cruickshank was born in Aberdeen in 1920 where he worked as bank clerk before enlisting in the Royal Artillery.

In early 1941 he volunteered for the Royal Air Force and gained his wings in July 1942. He joined 210 Squadron in March 1943 and flew Catalina flying boats. On the afternoon of July 17 1944 he took off from the flying boat base at Sullom Voe for a 14 hour patrol in Catalina JV 928. Whilst out on patrol U 347 was sighted on the surface and the flying boat engaged the German submarine in battle. In the engagement Cruickshank's navigator and bomb aimer were killed and his second

pilot and two other crew were wounded. Cruickshank himself was wounded in no less than 72 places, including two serious lung wounds. He carried on, dropping depth charges himself which finally sunk the enemy submarine. For most of the 5 ½ hour flight back Cruickshank was unconscious but insisted on landing the plane himself — and this operation was then itself delayed by over an hour due to unfavourable weather conditions. Upon landing his physical condition was so desperate he was given a blood transfusion in the plane but, miraculously, he survived to receive the Victoria Cross at Holyrood Palace on September 21 1944. This is reckoned to be the most outstanding action in Coastal Command history and one of the most commendable air force actions of the war.

BIBLIOGRAPHY

Beardmore, George: *Civilians at War*, London 1985
Calder, Angus: *The People's War*, London 1969
Churchill, Winston L. S.: *The Second World War*, London 1948-54
Ferguson, James D.: *The Story of Aberdeen Airport*, Glasgow 1984
Harris, Paul: *Glasgow at War*, Manchester 1986
Harrisson, Tom: *Living Through the Blitz*, London 1976
HMSO: *Front Line 1940—41; The Official Story of the Civil Defence of Britain*, 1942
Johnson, B. S.: *The Evacuees*, London 1968
Jones, R. V.: *Most Secret War*, London 1978
Keith, Alexander: *A Thousand Years of Aberdeen*, Aberdeen 1972
Lewis, Peter: *A People's War*, London 1986
Linklater, Eric: *The Highland Division*, London 1942
Odhams Press: *Ourselves in Wartime*, London n. d.
Schofield, B. B.: *The Russian Convoys*, London 1964
West, Nigel: *Unreliable Witness: Espionage Myths of the Second World War*, London 1984
Wyness, Fenton: *City by the Grey North Sea*, Aberdeen 1965

Newspaper files: *The Press & Journal, The Evening Express, Bon Accord*

Magazines: Contemporary issues of *The War Illustrated*, and *The War in Pictures*

Front cover photograph:
Wings for Victory Week, June 19—26 1943 and the parade passes the saluting dais at the Music Hall in Union Street

Back cover:
Hazlehead Park, July 1944, and there was an impressive march and demonstration by girls of the Women's Timber Corps for the amusement of Aberdonians on their 'Stay at Home' holidays.